Keith Lowe

Teaching Thomas

Editor *Pauletta Edwards*

Illustrator *Joan Gammans*

Project team: Ken Cripwell *World Health Organisation/ Institute of Education, London, UK.*
Dr Pauletta Edwards *University College Cardiff, UK.*
Shan Griffith-Pinna *Curriculum specialist.*
Colette Hawes *Language specialist*
Hugh Hawes *Institute of Education, London, UK.*
Dr Keith Lowe *Ministry of Education, Kingston, Jamaica.*
Augustine Veliath *Voluntary Health Association of India.*
Professor David Morley *Institute of Child Health, London, UK.*

LONGMAN

MAINLY FOR PARENTS AND TEACHERS

Children learn more in their first years than at
any other time in their lives. This is the story of
how one baby grows up and how his older
brother helps him to develop – to co-ordinate
his body, to learn language and to solve
problems.

It emphasises the importance of talking to
children, playing with them and making toys
and games to stimulate their physical and
mental growth. There are many practical
suggestions on toys which children can make
for their younger brothers and sisters, both at
home and in school, as well as on games they
can play.

Pearson Education Limited
Edinburgh Gate, Harlow,
Essex CM20 2JE, England
and Associated Companies throughout the world.

First published 1985
Fifteenth impression 2005

Set in Univers Medium (Lasercomp)
Printed in Malaysia, PA

ISBN 0-582-89512-X

The little fellow

"You see this little fellow? He is my brother, Thomas. He is very useful to me," said Samuel.

"Useful," his friend, Joseph, said. "He doesn't look useful. He is too little."

"He dresses me," said Samuel.

"What? You mean, you dress him."

"No, he dresses me. He brought me these clothes."

"I don't believe it!"

"Let me explain. He is a big boy for his age, isn't he?"

"Yes, he is quite big," said Joseph.

"He is happy and he talks well, doesn't he?" Samuel said.

"Sometimes I wish he would stop talking! — He is always asking questions. Why? Why? Why?"

"He is very active too, isn't he?" Samuel said. "He jumps and runs and throws balls."

"Yes," Joseph answered. "He is very active. Yesterday he jumped down from a tree and ran away with my ball."

"Yes, but he threw it back, didn't he?"

"Yes, he did. But tell me how he dressed you."

Samuel tells his story

"I am eleven now," Samuel said. "I was seven when Thomas was born. Mama said to me: "Samuel, you have to help me with this baby! I want him to grow up strong and healthy and happy. I want him to learn to talk well. I want him to be ready for school when he is five. Your little sister can help too, but you must be my special helper. You know I am very busy."

I know she is very busy. She is a nurse for sick children. She works in a hospital and she has to work late in the evening.

5

"Sometimes I will not have time to play with Baby, but that will not matter," said Mama. "He is your baby too, so you can play with him. You will be my special helper and I will give you a present each time Baby does something important. When he learns to sit up, I will give you some shorts. When he learns to walk, I will give you some shoes. When he learns to talk, I will give you a shirt. When he begins to count, I will give you a special present."

"But, Mama!" I said. "You don't need to give me presents. I want to play with Baby but I don't know how babies play."

"I will help you," said Mama. "I will tell you what to do. Do you remember how you learned to play football?"

"Yes, Mama."

"Do you remember all the things you had to learn? How to kick and how to pass the ball? Do you remember how you watched the other boys? You did what they did and you tried and tried."

"Yes."

"It is a little like that with Thomas. He has to learn many things. He has to learn to use *his body*. He has to learn to use his arms and legs, his hands and feet. He must learn to make big movements, like sitting and walking. He must learn to make little clever movements like holding or catching or putting on his shoes. He must learn to use his eyes and ears, his taste and smell. He must learn to use his *senses*," said Mama.

"What a lot he has to learn!" I said.

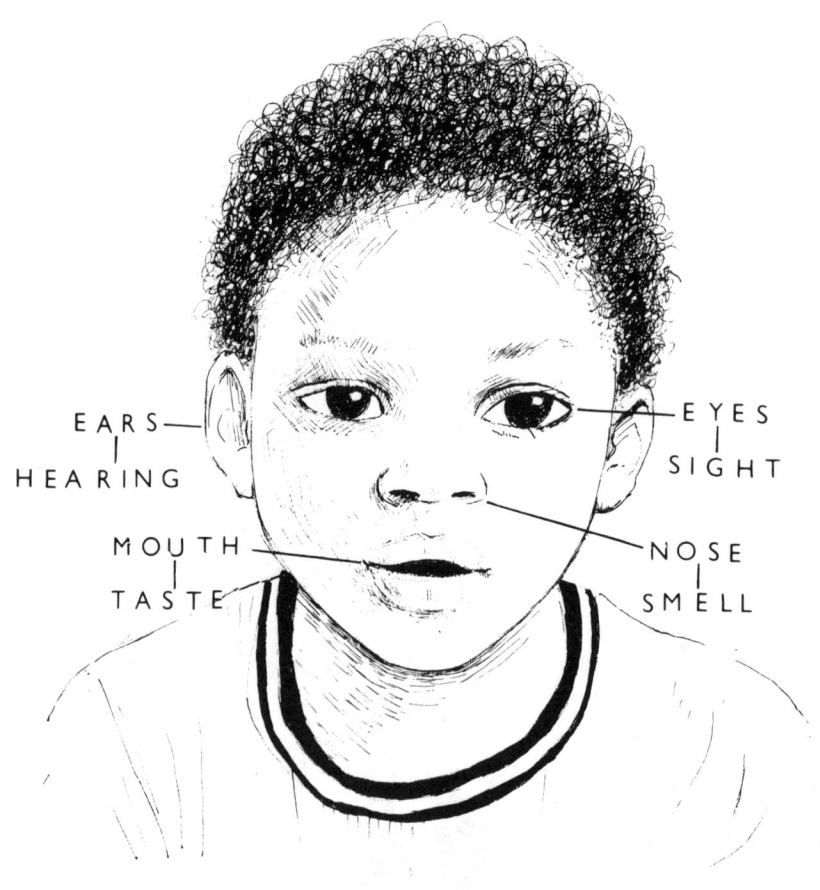

EARS — HEARING

EYES — SIGHT

MOUTH — TASTE

NOSE — SMELL

"That is not all," said Mama. "He must learn to think. He must learn to use language. He must learn to talk and learn to listen. He must learn words and how to put words together. He must learn to ask questions."

"Can he learn all that?" I asked.

"Yes," said my mother. "He can learn it all if you help him and if we all help him."

"Yes, I will help," I said. "And you will help me. Will anyone else help me?"

"The other children can help you," said my mother. "They can play games with the baby. They can talk to him. Your sister can help you. The shopkeepers can help you. They can give you many things they don't want. You can collect them for Baby to play with. The school can help. They can teach you how to make toys and games and books for Baby to play with. These toys and games will not cost any money."

That is how I began learning how to play with Thomas.

When Thomas was very small

When Thomas was very small he slept most of the time.
When he woke up he cried. then he sucked milk from my
mother. "We must always give Baby breast milk," she said.
"Powder milk is not good for babies."

He drank and then he made wind noises. Then he wet
and then he slept.

"That baby doesn't play," I said. "You can't play with
that baby."

"Pick him up," said Mama. "Hold him. Rock him. Sing
to him. He likes it,"

He liked it. He didn't cry. He went to sleep.

After a few weeks I saw that Thomas watched moving things. One day I held a red flower in my hand. I moved it slowly in front of Thomas. He watched the flower all the time. He liked it.

Soon he began to smile. My mother smiled at him and he smiled at her. He smiled at his sisters and he smiled at me. My mother played a game with him. She hid her face with a cloth. She took the cloth away and smiled at Thomas. He smiled back. Mama hid her face again. Then she took the cloth away and smiled at Thomas. He smiled and made his happy noises. "You do it," said my mother. I did it and Thomas smiled. That was the first time I played with him.

One day my mother stood behind Thomas and clapped her hands. He moved. "Why did you do that?" I asked. "I wanted to see if he can hear," said Mama. "A few babies can't hear very well. If they can't hear, we must take them to the doctor. Thomas hears very well."

Thomas liked different sounds. He liked me to talk to him and sing to him. One day I took an old tin with a lid on it. I put beans in the tin and shook it. They rattled. Thomas smiled and smiled. That was the first toy I made for him.

After three months he began to hold up his hands and reach for things. He reached for everything he could see.

"Why don't you make him some more toys?" said my mother.

I made something for him to look at called a *mobile*. My mobile looked like this.

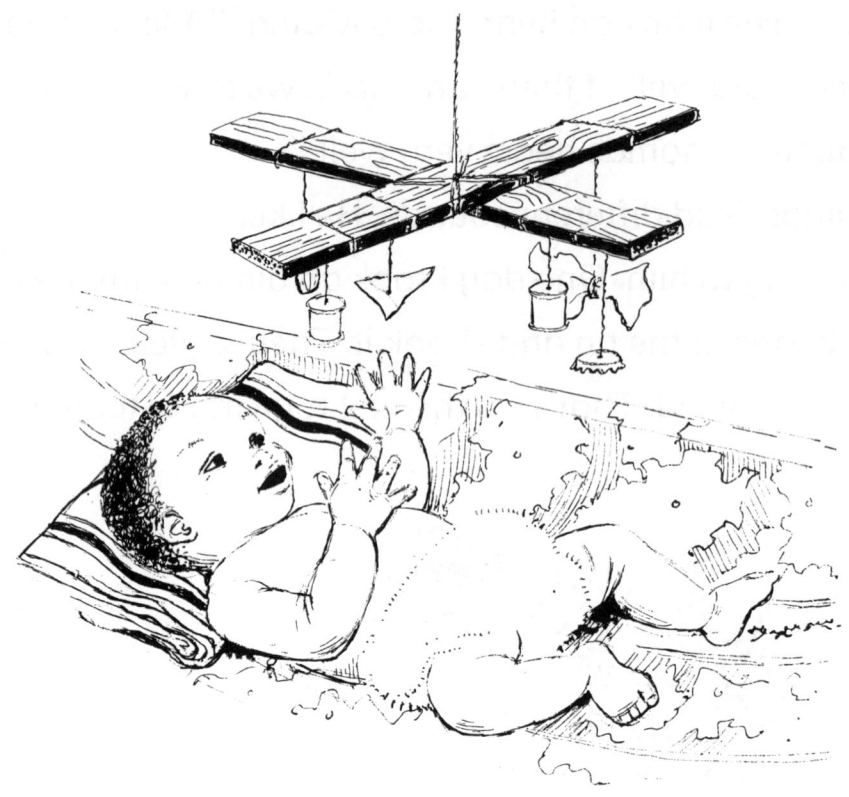

I made it with two pieces of wood and some string. First I coloured the pieces of wood. Then I tied them together in a cross. Then I found things to hang from the wood. Thomas watched the mobile all the time. He smiled and laughed.

Then I had another idea. I went to my friend in the market and asked her to help me. She gave me bottle tops, a plastic bottle and some old cotton reels. I put them on a string and hung them across the cot where Thomas lay. Thomas reached for the string and laughed.

Thomas did not spend too much time in the cot. My mother and my auntie often carried him round on their backs. He liked being carried. He liked being near to us. He liked us to talk and sing to him. We played singing games with his fingers and toes. "One little chicken. Two little chickens. Three little chickens . . ." He laughed and laughed.

He liked my father to hold him and throw him up in the air.

Sometimes we put him down on a mat. We put him inside or outside in a shady place, safe from ants and mango flies. Sometimes we put him on his front. He kicked and moved his arms and legs. He smiled and laughed.

When Thomas was five months old my mother said: "He will soon want to sit up." She showed me how to hold his hands so that he could pull himself up. He liked it. Every day he wanted me to play like that. Every day he needed less help. Each time he tried I said: "Well done, Thomas!"

Then one day he sat up all by himself. He smiled and laughed. He seemed to be saying: "Look, Samuel. I have learnt to sit."

"Look, Mama. Thomas is sitting up," I said.

"So he is," said Mama. "You are both very clever."

Next morning there was a parcel on my bed. In it was the new pair of shorts my mother promised me. That was how Thomas started to dress me.

Thomas learns to walk

This is how I got my pair of shoes. They were strong shoes. I could run fast in them!

"One day Thomas will run fast like me," I said to myself. "But before he can run he must walk. Before he can walk he must stand. Before he can stand he must crawl."

"When Thomas walks I will give you a pair of shoes," my mother said. "He will need a lot of help to walk. But don't forget to talk to him too and help him to talk. Don't forget he has to learn many things. The more you play with him the more he will learn."

I looked at Thomas. His legs looked fat and strong. "This little fellow will get me a new pair of shoes before long," I thought. Mama saw me looking at his legs. She said: "What about his arms?"

"He doesn't need arms to walk," I said.

"Oh, he does!" Mama said. He needs his arms to keep his balance when he is walking. He needs his hands to hold on when he is learning to walk."

"What is balance?" I asked.

"Balance stops you falling over," Mama said. "Like when you ride a bicycle. That is balance." Mama stood on a small tin and put her arms out. "Look!" she said. "That is balance."

I gave Thomas things to do with his hands. I found an empty paint tin and two old spoons. Thomas liked to hit the tin with the spoons. Bang, bang, bang! Then I took the spoons and hit like a drummer. BING, BANG, BING!

"That is how to drum, Thomas. Do you want to become a great drummer?"

Thomas couldn't answer my questions, but I asked him a lot of questions. Mama said: "Talk to him like a big person," So I didn't often talk baby-talk.

Thomas liked to hold things in his hands. Sometimes he banged the thing on the floor. I went to the carpenter one day. I got bits of wood that the carpenter didn't need. He called them blocks. I made sure they were smooth and safe for Thomas. I gave these blocks to Thomas. He banged them on the floor. I showed him how to put the blocks in the paint tin. Soon he could do this by himself. He put the blocks in the tin and he took them out. He did this again and again. I didn't think it was much fun, but Thomas liked it.

I had to help Thomas to crawl. This is what I did. I put him on the mat and I put the tin and the spoons near him. He put out his hand, but he couldn't reach them. He had to move himself. He tried and tried. After many tries he moved himself. Then I put the things a little further away from him. When he reached them, I moved the things away again. We played this game day after day. Thomas always crawled and then stopped. He seemed to say: "Shall I move an arm or leg next?

After some weeks he moved his arms and legs together. He moved like this: left arm, left leg, right arm, right leg. He didn't have to stop and think any more.

One day Thomas held on to the leg of a table and pulled himself up. There he was, standing on two legs. "Well done, Thomas! You are a man now!" I said. "You are not an animal with four legs any more." As soon as I said this, Thomas let go and fell back on his bottom. Plop!

Next day he did it again and the next day too. He could hold on and stand up longer and longer.

Next I helped Thomas to stand up by himself. This is what I did. At first I gave him my two hands to hold and he stood up. After several tries I gave him only one hand. He fell back on his bottom sometimes, but he fell less often. Then one day Thomas let go of my hand and stood up by himself. "Hurrah, Thomas! You can stand up by yourself now!" As soon as I said this, he fell back on his bottom. Plop!

"His legs aren't strong enough yet," I told Mama. "His legs are all right," Mama said. "It is his balance. He will learn to balance."

"But he must also learn to put one foot in front of the other, mustn't he?" I asked.

"Oh, yes," Mama said. "Thomas is ready to walk. Give him some help."

I took his two hands and helped him to step towards me. We did this several times. Sometimes I let go of his hands and he fell. But he got up and tried again. What a hero!

Then one day he got up all by himself and took one step. Ah! Then he took another. Ah! "Welcome to the human race, boy," cried Mama. As soon as she said this, Thomas fell back on his bottom. Plop!

The next day Mama came home with a new pair of shoes, not for the new walker but for me!

Thomas learns to talk

At first Thomas only walked one or two steps. Then he fell on his bottom. Plop! Then he began to walk and not fall down. Soon he could walk quickly. Then he began to run. He ran everywhere. He ran in and out of the house. He ran round the house. He broke everything. One day he broke a cup, a plate and a pot. That is when we called him Thomas Crash!

My mother laughed at our name. "You must be careful of Thomas Crash," she said. "You must watch him all the time. He will get out on the road. He will run to the fire and get burnt. He will pick up things and put them in his mouth. You must make him plenty of toys to play with."

I made a lot of toys for Thomas Crash. I made a roller he could push. I made a ball of banana fibre. I made a lorry he could pull.

Then I went to the tailor and asked for bits of cloth he didn't want. He gave me big bits and little bits.

My friend, Mary, made a dog for Thomas. She made it in her sewing classes at school. She made the outside with the big bits of cloth. She put the little bits of cloth inside. It was a blue and yellow dog. Thomas loved his dog and took it to bed every day. He held it and talked to it. Sometimes he tried to eat it.

"We don't eat dogs," I told him.

Sometimes I think Thomas will become a builder when he grows up. "He will be like the builder in our village," I told Joseph. "He built a very big house last year. He built it very quickly and it fell down. Thomas is like him. He is always building."

I went to my friend, the carpenter and he gave me more blocks. I went to my friend, the shopkeeper and he gave me empty boxes. Thomas put one thing on top of another. They always fell down.

"He is learning to use his hands," my mother said. "He is learning to balance the pieces of wood. He is learning to *feel* the different shapes."

I don't know when Thomas said his first real word. He talked a lot, but he had his own words. I didn't understand them. Then he began to say words like "Mama" and "Dada". Then one day he said: "Sa-sa", and laughed at me. I was very happy. "I am going to teach you to talk," I said. "I am going to teach you to talk all the time, like my teacher."

So I taught Thomas to talk. I showed him things. I said: "There is the lorry." "There is a cow." "There is the dog." I sang songs and played singing games with him. I sang:

"This is the way we clap our hands.

This is the way we wash our face."

Thomas tried to do these things. He tried and tried.

Then I hid things where he could find them easily. I said: "Where is the ball?" Thomas found them very soon. When he found the things I was very happy with him and said the name over many times. "There is the ball, Thomas. You found the ball. You are a clever boy." Thomas said: "Ball, ball, BALL," very loudly. He loved this game. I got tired of playing it.

Mama told Thomas stories. She told him little stories with the words he knew. She told him about cars and about cows. She told him about me and about my sisters. She was always talking to him.

I made a book for Thomas at school. I made it out of old pieces of cardboard. The shopkeeper gave them to me. I cut pictures from the newspaper. There were cars and a house and pictures of children. I made glue with cassava flour and water. Then I stuck the pictures on the cardboard and tied the pieces together with string, like this.

I showed my book to Thomas. I pointed to the pictures and told stories about them. Soon Thomas knew all the pictures. He said: "Car, house, cow, Father." He called all men Father.

Thomas learnt a lot of words in our language. Every day he seemed to know another one. Then one day when Thomas was two, he started to put words together. He said: "Where is Jo-Jo come?"

"He is talking," I said to Mama. "He isn't just saying words. He is talking."

"So he is!" said Mama. "It is time you got your new shirt."

Thomas learns to count

"Well, Samuel," said Mama, "your brother Thomas can now say words. Next he must say numbers."

"Numbers?" I asked. "Do you mean 1, 2, 3, 4?" "Yes. Thomas must learn to count from one to ten." "Oh, he will have to go to school to do that," I said.

"No. You can teach him. When Thomas can count, I will give you some nice things."

"What nice things?" I asked. "You'll see," she said.

"Oh, no!" I thought. "I can't do this. This will take too long. When will Thomas ever learn to count?" He seemed very clever to me before. Now he didn't seem to know very much. He never even knew when his nose was running.

In fact, Thomas liked to play in mud like a pig. I didn't allow him to play in mud. It made him dirty like a pig. Then one day Mama saw him crawling in the mud. She didn't take him out. She gave him an empty can and an old spoon. Thomas took up mud in the spoon and put it in the can. Mama emptied the can. Thomas put mud in it again. I went to play with them and I pressed the mud down into the can too. Then I turned the can upside down. Out came a nice round cake. Thomas Crash smashed the mud cake with his spoon, but I made another cake.

33

"That is enough now, Thomas," Mama said. She picked him up and bathed him. She said: "Thomas can play in the mud if he has a wash straight afterwards."

I made many mud cakes for Thomas. I made other shapes with mud. One day my sister mixed the mud well and made a little bowl out of the mud. She let it dry in the sun and it became very hard.

"You see!" I told Thomas. "You can play in mud like a pot maker instead of a pig."

Thomas made a funny sound like a pig. Was that his answer? May be he understood what I said. He understood a lot of words. He answered yes or no when we asked him questions. But he didn't know any numbers.

We all talked a lot to Thomas. Mama named the parts of his body when she bathed him. So he learnt these words. Sister recited rhymes for him when she carried him on her back. I pointed to the sun and moon and called these words. Soon he was pointing and calling to the sun and moon.

Once I got a bucket of dry sand. Thomas filled one can with sand and then he poured it from that can into another one. Then he poured it back into the other can. Once I gave him a bucket of water. He did the same thing. He filled one can. Then he poured it into another can. Funny fellow!

Mama said: "Thomas learns a lot when he does this."
Funny Mama!

Thomas was three years old. He always wanted me to play with him. He cried if I didn't. I was ten years old. I wanted to play with other boys of my own age. Why didn't my little sister play with him? Mama said: "Samuel, my son, play with little Thomas. At this age he is learning very much."

"What?" my sister said: "He isn't at school yet!"

"How can he learn when I play with him?" I asked.

"Because babies learn by playing," Mama said. "For them, playing is learning."

"Is this true?" I asked myself. "My mother is a nurse. She isn't a teacher."

So I went to my teacher. I asked her: "Is it true that you can learn by playing?"

"Oh, yes," she said. "If you play clever games, like word games and number games, they teach you to think. Don't we play clever games in class?"

"Yes," I said. "But what about my brother Thomas? He is only a baby. He isn't in any class. Can he learn by playing?"

"Oh, yes," she said. "Your baby brother can learn a lot from play before he comes to school."

PLAY WITH BABIES
TALK TO THEM
SING TO THEM
MAKE THEM TOYS
AND GAMES
BE HAPPY WITH THEM
HELP THEM WALK
HELP THEM TALK

At school we make things for babies to play with. One day we made a picture on a piece of cardboard. We made a picture of some ripe bananas. Then we cut the cardboard picture into four parts. I took the parts home and put them together to make the picture.

"Look, Thomas. See, banana!" Thomas looked. He smiled. He loved to eat bananas. He touched the picture. I took up the parts and mixed them up. Then there was no picture. Thomas looked at me. "Don't worry," I said. "I can make the picture again."

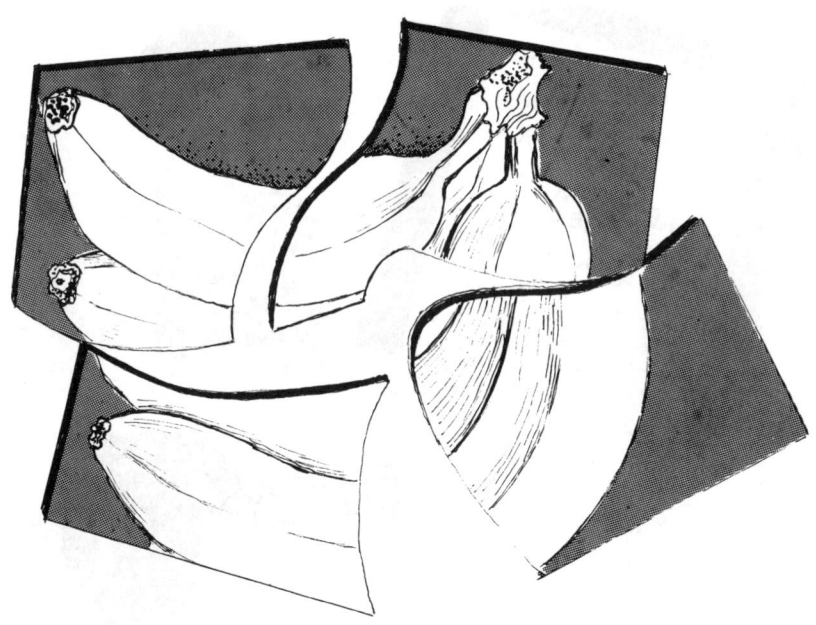

I fitted the parts together and made the bananas come back. Thomas smiled. Then I mixed up the pieces. I said to Thomas: "Make the bananas come back." He picked up the parts, but he couldn't make the picture.

I asked my teacher about it. She said: "Thomas isn't ready to do that. First he must learn to fit things. He must learn to see shapes."

I cut more cardboard into round shapes and square shapes. I showed Thomas that round shapes couldn't fit with square shapes. I showed him how square shapes fitted with square shapes. I went to the carpenter again. I got more smooth blocks. I also got some round bits of wood. I made things for Thomas out of the bits of wood. I made a road, a bridge and a house.

Sometimes I left Thomas to play with the wood bits by himself. One day we saw him trying to put a big bit of wood into my shoe. He tried and tried, but the wood was much too big. Thomas didn't know the size of things.

I held up the wood bit and said: "Big." Then I held up the shoe and said: "Small."

"Very good, Samuel," said my mother. "Thomas must say the words "big" and "small". But he must also learn what these words mean." She said: "Get a lot of boxes for Thomas to play with." So I got a lot of match boxes, cigarette boxes and boxes of all sizes. Thomas put things in the boxes. He put boxes inside boxes. He began to learn when something was bigger or smaller than another thing. He began to learn if one thing could fit into another. He also learnt how much of one thing could fit into another thing. He was beginning to think about things.

We all tried to teach Thomas to count. We tried all the ways we knew. I used the wood bits. I picked up one and said "one" and put it aside. I picked up another and said "two" and put it beside the first one. I did this until I got to five.

My sister sang a counting song to him. She sang it many times. Thomas could sing a little bit of the song.

My mother counted his fingers and toes aloud.

ONE....TWO....THREE

When she fed him, she counted each spoonful aloud.

It took a long time, but one day Thomas counted quickly from one to five. Then very slowly he said: "Six . . . seven . . . eight . . . nine . . . ten."

"Hurrah, Thomas!" I cried. "Mother, Thomas can count!"

"So he can," Mama said.

I thought Mama was going to give me a new shirt. And she did! She also gave me new shorts and new shoes, a belt and a pair of socks. She gave my little sister a new dress!

We wore our new things the next Sunday and everyone said: "How good you look!" Except Thomas. He just smiled. He looked very happy. He had dressed me!

"What about Thomas?" I asked. "What will he get?"

"I'll tell you some news," Mama said. "In six months we are going to have a new baby. The new baby can dress Thomas!"

Two puzzle games

You need 16 pieces of red cardboard 15 cm by 5 cm. Many children can help to make the pieces. Then it will be quick and easy to make.

On each piece of cardboard write one sentence. Write on one side only. The other side of the cardboard is blank. Here are the 16 sentences:

Thomas drinks milk from his mother

Thomas watches the red flower

Thomas hears Mama clap her hands

Thomas watches the mobile

Thomas sits up and laughs

Thomas puts blocks in the tin

Thomas takes his first steps

Thomas runs about and breaks things

Thomas gets his blue and yellow dog

Thomas tries to build with blocks

Thomas looks at his book and says words

Thomas puts words together

Thomas makes shapes with mud

Thomas plays with water and sand

Thomas puts wooden shapes together

Thomas learns to count

Now cut each piece into 3 pieces like this:

Thomas   sits up and   laughs

Make the cuts in each shape different:

Thomas   takes   his first steps

When the pieces are all cut you can start to play.

First game

2, 3 or 4 children can play this game. Put all the pieces face downwards like this:

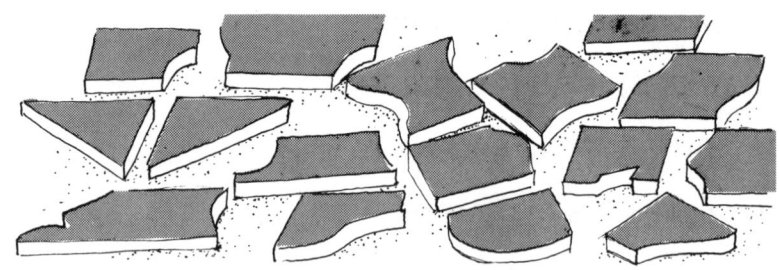

The writing doesn't show.

The first player takes two shapes. If the shapes fit together, he can take another piece and another. He takes pieces until he gets a piece that does not fit. Then he must stop. Then the next person plays. A player can only have five seconds (count slowly to five) to choose a piece. If he doesn't get the right piece, he puts his piece face upwards like this:

The next player can choose two pieces. He may choose either those facing upwards or those facing downwards. Soon more and more pieces will be face upwards on the table. Then it will be easier to choose. The player with the most pieces at the end of the game is the winner.

Second game

All the pieces are put face upwards on the table. Children work in pairs. Each pair has to put the 16 pieces together. Then they have to arrange them in the correct order.

This is the same order as the list. This is the same way as Thomas learnt them. One child is time-keeper. He turns his back on the two players. Then he counts very slowly. You have won if you finish quickest!

Things to do

1   Make the toys that Samuel made for your own little sister and brother. Think of new toys.

2   Play the games Samuel played with your sister and brother. Think of new games.

3   Make books like Samuel made and show to the young children.

4   Draw pictures of Thomas or your own small sister or brother:

> learning to crawl
> learning to walk
> breaking things
> playing with mud, sand or water
> putting shapes together

5   Go to shopkeepers in your town or village. Collect things for making toys and games. Give them to your own brothers and sisters or to other little children. Let older people see them first to make sure they are safe.

6   Play acting or guessing games with your friends. Be a little child learning some important thing. Let them guess what you are doing.

7   Write a story about your own little sister or brother.

REMEMBER

- Help Baby to grow up.
- Older children can help.
- Baby learns better with help.
- Children learn quicker too.
- They do better at school.
- Children need help to
    - use their bodies well
    - learn language
    - learn to think.
- Always talk with them.
- Sing to them.
- Be happy with them.
- Always play with children.
- Give them toys and games.
- Watch over children.
- Keep them from harm.

The CHILD-to-child stories are edited by Pauletta Edwards, illustrated by Joan Gammans and written by a group of teachers and doctors:

Ken Cripwell
Pauletta Edwards
Shân Griffith Pinna
Colette Hawes
Hugh Hawes
Keith Lowe
Augustine Veliath
David Morley

What is CHILD - to - child?

CHILD-to-child is an International Programme which teaches and encourages children of school age to concern themselves with the health, welfare and general development of their younger pre-school brothers and sisters and of other younger children in their community.

Each of the stories in this series of readers is based on the CHILD-to-child concept of one child helping another.

It is hoped too that children will read these stories to their younger brothers and sisters thus giving practical expression to the CHILD-to-child idea.

THE PUBLISHERS RECEIVED ASSISTANCE IN THE PRODUCTION OF THIS BOOK AS A LOW COST EDITION FROM THE **SWEDISH INTERNATIONAL DEVELOPMENT AUTHORITY**.